I0813784

YOU ONLY LIVE ONCE

First published in 2025 by OH
An Imprint of HEADLINE PUBLISHING GROUP LIMITED

1

Disclaimer:
This book has not been licensed, approved, sponsored, or endorsed by Drake.

Drake is a registered trademark

Cataloguing in Publication Data is available from the British Library

ISBN 978-1-03542-304-0

Compiled and written by: Malcolm Croft
Editorial: Saneaah Muhammad
Designed and typeset in Avenir by: Andy Jones
Project manager: Russell Porter
Production: Arlene Lestrade
Printed and bound in Dubai

Headline's policy is to use papers that are natural, renewable and recyclable products and made from wood grown in well-managed forests and other controlled sources. The logging and manufacturing processes are expected to conform to the environmental regulations of the country of origin.

HEADLINE PUBLISHING GROUP LIMITED
An Hachette UK Company
Carmelite House, 50 Victoria Embankment, London EC4Y 0DZ

The authorised representative in the EEA is Hachette Ireland, 8 Castlecourt Centre, Dublin 15, D15 XTP3, Ireland (email: info@hbgi.ie)

www.headline.co.uk www.hachette.co.uk

YOU ONLY LIVE ONCE

THE LITTLE GUIDE TO DRAKE

UNOFFICIAL AND UNAUTHORIZED

CONTENTS

INTRODUCTION

It's been over 10 years since 2015 – the "Year of Drake" – when Canada's biggest musical export was everywhere, as ubiquitous as he was multi-talented and, without a doubt, the most famous musician on the planet. In the five years before that, and with the arrival of his jaw-dropping debut album *Thank Me Later* (2010), Drake conquered every corner of the globe, utterly smashing chart records everywhere he went – he remains the most-streamed male artist in the world, even today – and breaking the Internet with a veritable feast of meme-worthy interviews and his iconic collection of sweaters.

As the first ever bi-racial Canadian Jewish child actor turned rap star, Aubrey Drake Graham has always been a unique proposition. (Go on: name another bi-racial Canadian Jewish child actor turned rap star?) But, as the rapper himself has gone to great pains himself to say, where he is from and what he looks like is only a small part of his staggering global success. His music, like him, is in a league of its own. Simply put, there's no one else like him in the game. He's an artist that transcends genres and defies conventions, mixing searing honesty and vulnerability with tremendous self-confidence and authenticity, all over the top of delicious beats and flawless flows. Like him or not, he's the real deal.

From child actor to high school dropout to iconic giant of popular culture, Drake has been a mesmerising mononym in the mainstream, bigger than even Beyoncé (maybe), bringing together rap, hip-hop and pop all under one very entrepreneurial roof... and selling more than 170 million albums in the process.

Now, as he approaches 40, this little guide celebrates Aubrey Drake Graham in the best way possible: through his own wit and wisdom. Of which there's a lot, judging by the next 192 pages. This tiny tome is a celebration of the man, the myth and the music and his reputation for being one of the most innovative and entertaining rappers of his generation, no matter what Kendrick Lamar may say to the contrary.

Enjoy!

CHAPTER ONE

SO LONG JIMMY BROOKS

For seven years, from the age of 15, Drake juggled an acting career on the popular Canadian teen soap drama *Degrassi: The Next Generation* with his burning desire to create game-changing rap and hip-hop.

The music won, and the world hasn't been the same since...

The new version of Fresh Prince frequently referred to as Mr. Big Dreams... the only rapper up north that could claim king, but won't because I always let the people decide. A self-proclaimed king is merely a peasant with a big mouth.

”

Drake, on who he is, when asked "Who the fuck are you?", interview with Leslie Woods, *WRG Magazine*, 2006.

I know that Aubrey Drake Graham is not hood. I'm not a gangster, I don't have no desire to be hard. I will talk to you about real situations that I have really been through. I will give you pieces of my life, hoping that you will give me time in yours. I'm not afraid to go to the States and say I'm from Toronto. As a rapper, what you'll always get from me is a variety of emotions. Whenever you listen to my CD, whether you're the hardest dude or the bitterest cat, I'll give you a real story to think about. Just to sit back and be like, 'Damn yo, that's a trip.'

Drake, on his mission statement to the world, interview with *HipHopCanada*, July 12, 2006.

My name is Drake. I started in 2008, I came all the way from Toronto, Canada. The year is now 2025, and Drizzy Drake is very much still alive.

Drake, his first live remarks after the release of Kendrick Lamar's 'Not Like Us' diss track, Perth, Australia, February 4, 2025.

I had an audition for a TV show that ultimately shaped my life, and before my audition, I went to this kid's house. And out of a desire to be accepted, I succumbed to peer pressure, and I got high with these kids right before my audition. I kind of wonder if maybe I'm still high and this is just me playing out my ideal life!

Drake, on being high before his infamous audition for *Degrassi: The Next Generation,* promo video for the It's All a Blur tour, 2023.

My dad was in jail for two years and he shared a cell with this dude who didn't really have anyone to speak to. So, he used to share his phone time with this dude. At the time I was 16, and this dude would always rap to me over the phone. He would call me and we would just rap to each other. After while I started to get into it and I started to write my own shit down. Eventually I learned the art of making a song and wanted to be in music.

”

Drake, on how he first got into rapping, interview with Damien Scott, *Complex*, May 30, 2009.

October 24, 1986

The day Drake was born. Cyndi Lauper's 'True Colours' was No.1 on the U.S. charts and Whitney Houston's debut album was No.1 on the album charts.

Degrassi was never something I saw as potentially ruining a music career. It was a great TV show. It had a cult following.

Drake, on the *Degrassi: Next Generation* TV show he appeared on from 2001 to 2008, interview with Amos Barshad, *Heeb*, June 18, 2010.

At first, I wanted to make the rapper's rap album, to prove that I'm one of the best. And then I realized, like, you know what? Fuck you.

Drake, on proving his talent to people when he has nothing he needs to prove, interview with Elliot Wilson, *Respect*, September 13, 2019.

Music was part of the reason I was kicked off the show, *Degrassi*. Back then, I'd spend a full day on set and then go to the studio to make music until 4 or 5 a.m. I'd sleep in my dressing room and then be in front of the cameras again by 9 a.m. Eventually, they realized I was juggling two professions and told me I had to choose. I chose this life.

”

Drake, on juggling two careers while acting in *Degrassi: The New Generation*, interview with Lynn Hirschberg, *W Magazine*, October 15, 2015

Coin me as mainstream or pop, man, I don't care. But I make real hip-hop records.

Drake, on being a genuine hip-hop artist, interview with Chris Lee, *Los Angeles Times*, June 14, 2010.

"I know my sound. I make records to fuck to."

Drake, on his signature sound, interview with *Complex*, January 25, 2010.

The three biggest misconceptions about me are that I'm a cocky asshole because I'm a famous male rapper, that any part of me wants to be gangster or hood, and that I grew up rich.

Drake, on his signature sound, interview with *Complex*, January 25, 2010.

I'm so solid on who I am, who I've been from day one, who I am now, the music I make, the decisions I make. I used to be so tuned into what people had to say about me, their little comments and shit on the radio and online. I just don't care anymore. I just don't give a fuck.

”

Drake, on no longer worrying about what people say about him, interview with Damien Scott, *Complex*, November 15, 2011.

Acting was all I wanted to do, at first. I loved music. I just didn't necessarily believe in music being the focus right away.

”

Drake, on acting, interview with Claire Hoffman, *GQ*, April 13, 2012.

I have a fan base that some people say is equal to that of signed artists, maybe even more. *Degrassi* is shown in 40 million homes in the US and spectators say that I would be the perfect person to sign because I have a large fan base. I feel like if I was to come out with an album, with the right publicity and of course the great music, I could not see it failing.

”

Drake, on trying to get his first album made, interview with *HipHopCanada*, July 12, 2006.

If you're a truly multi-layered artist, you can make it from anywhere. Do it the way I did it. Do it from where you're at. If you have the music, that's all it takes.

”

Drake, on not worrying where you're from, interview with Alexander Iadarola, *Fader*, June 24, 2015.

I am not the first person in my family to embrace music but I would like to become the first one to be an icon.

Drake, on his career aspirations, interview with *HipHopCanada*, July 12, 2006.

We were very poor, like broke. The only money I had coming in was off of Canadian TV, which isn't that much money when you break it down. A season of Canadian television is under a teacher's salary, I'll tell you that much. It's definitely not something to go fucking get.

”

Drake, on his *Degrassi: The Next Generation* salary (roughly $40,000 a year), interview with Damien Scott, Complex, November 15, 2011.

Music has always been a major part of my life. My uncle played bass for Prince [and] my father, Dennis Graham, wrote for Al Green and drummed for Jerry Lee Lewis. I've always been around great music.

Drake, on his high pedigree musical heritage, interview with Damien Scott, *Complex*, May 30, 2009.

There's times where I'm sitting around looking for three or four words. The hardest moments, the most difficult ones, in songwriting, are when you're looking for four words with the right melody and the right cadence. I pray for that. I'll take that over anything – I'll take that over sex, partying. Give me that feeling.

Drake, on his passion (and frustration) for songwriting, interview with Leon Neyfakh, *Fader*, September 24, 2015.

Me and my dad are friends. We're cool. I'll never be disappointed again, because I don't expect anything anymore from him. I just let him exist, and that's how we get along. We laugh. We have drinks together. But I spent too many nights looking by the window, seeing if the car was going to pull up. And the car never came.

Drake, on his rocky relationship with his absent father, interview with Claire Hoffman, *GQ*, April 13, 2012.

I was friends with this kid that would put you on the spot all the time. I guess he read my rhyme books at my house and one day he just put me on blast at school. He told this kid I wanted to battle him and it became this big thing. So I went home and wrote all these rhymes for him. I came to school the next day and killed the guy. From there I just started getting into rapping and becoming comfortable with myself.

”

Drake, on his first rap battle at school, interview with *Vibe*, February 26, 2009.

“

I don’t want to limit my music to people based on their race and/or age. That’s why I don’t really put a lot of swearing in my music. I want everybody to be able to enjoy it. Being bi-racial and being young and Canadian allows me to try and cover all the bases and expand my fan base to a level that has yet to be seen. I want everybody to feel comfortable with vibing with Drake.

”

Drake, on being perfectly placed to make an impact with his music, interview with *HipHopCanada*, July 12, 2006.

Coming from Canada, and a TV show, I kept thinking, If I can really do something different, I may be regarded as the one of the first crossover-from-film-to-music people to really be looked at as an artist.

Drake, on breaking the mould in order to break through from his past, interview with *Vibe*, February 26, 2009.

I can't really say I left that show. One day we came in and all the names were just changed on the dressing rooms. Everyone got cut. We go upstairs and it's like, 'Who are all these people auditioning in the front?' They owe us a lot of money. The amount of loyalty, the years we put in with these people… they did us foul. As far as the producers go, I don't talk to anybody over there.

Drake, on the end of his time on the TV show *Degrassi: The Next Generation*, interview with *Vibe*, February 26, 2009.

It's a toss-up between three sweaters. I'd say one would be obviously the OVO Owl Sweater. I can wear it repetitively and no one calls me out on it. I have a cashmere Hermes sweater that I love. Lastly, any of my Missoni sweaters. I don't give a fuck what anybody says about my Missoni sweaters! Fuck you, if you don't like my sweater!

Drake, on his infamous and iconic love of a good sweater, interview with Mark Anthony Green, *GQ*, November 11, 2011.

Before people had heard my music they were like, 'So you're really going to be a rapper? That's really going to be your thing?' Especially around that time, that dope boy rap was really popping. People were wondering what the hell I was going to do. And it took me a while to find my sound.

Drake, on his aspirations to be a rapper while still appearing as an actor on *Degrassi: The Next Generation*, interview with Vibe, February 26, 2009.

"

I have some fame from *Degrassi*, but I am right at the bottom of my music career and trying to get meetings. That's why I respect people that are successful in the music business because you really have to build it from the ground up. Acting is sort of laid out for you, whereas in the music business you have to make the phone calls, go through the pressure, go to the studio, make sure all your shit is on point. It's a real process and it's taking a lot of my time right now.

"

Drake, on the difference between being an actor and a musician, interview with *HipHopCanada*, July 12, 2006.

CHAPTER TWO

FRESH PRINCE OF TORONTO

Canada's proudest son, Drake is forever flowing about his love of his hometown Toronto and how it inspired him and is infused into his iconic sound.

As rap's Mr Nice Guy, Drake is flying the Canadian flag for all to see. All hail Drake, Canadian royalty and the north's biggest musical export of the 21st century...

I constantly ask myself: Will I ever be able to excite people the way I did when the Internet was going crazy, back when fans first felt like they had a piece of Drake that no one else had, and they wanted to share it with your friends? Is there an album or song I can make now that's good enough to get people that excited again?

Drake, on trying to recapture the magic of 2009, before he was famous, interview with Michael Paterniti, *GQ*, June 18, 2013.

"

I'm always thinking, How do I top what I've done? How do I make this thing stronger? I ask myself, 'Why does Adele's album go diamond, and how do I do that? How do I create art that makes minds stretch further?' I want to give many, many people many, many moments before I'm gone. That's truly the art of what I do. It's the only goal.

"

Drake, on his long-term goal for his music, interview with Lynn Hirschberg, *W Magazine*, October 15, 2015.

I plan to spend the rest of my life in Toronto. The talk, the smell, the sound that comes out of that city is home to me. When I think about the girls I want to get romantic with, it's a girl from Toronto who knows what I'm talking about when we drive around the city.

”

Drake, on his love of his hometown, interview with Lynn Hirschberg, *W Magazine*, October 15, 2015.

"

A new flow is absolutely the most crucial discovery in rap, to me. My main joy in life is praying that Noah '40' Shebib has a beat that I can do something that I've never done before.

"

Drake, on creating new flows with his producer and musical partner, "40", interview with Leon Neyfakh, *Fader*, September 24, 2015.

With Take Care, I solidified my lane, what I do, and the artist I am.

Drake, on the significance of his second studio album, interview with Elliot Wilson, *Respect*, September 13, 2019.

I'm mischievous but I've never been reckless. I'm calculated.

Drake, on Drake, interview with Claire Hoffman, *GQ*, April 13, 2012

June 15, 2010

The day Drake dropped his hotly-anticipated debut studio album, *Thank Me Later.*

The 14-track record features collabs with a feast of high-profile artists including Alicia Keys, Timbaland, Swizz Beatz, Nicki Minaj, Lil Wayne and Kanye West.

Drake's It's All A Blur 72-date tour of 2023 was the highest-grossing rap tour ever, amassing more than £320 million with 1.3 million tickets sold, beating his nemesis Kendrick Lamar to the title.

After Thank Me Later, I was in such demand at the time that I was almost disconnecting with what was going on around me. It was kind of hard to tap into the psyche of myself. I could still make great songs. But it was hard to give people a huge part of Aubrey at that time.

”

Drake, on his rapid rise to fame following the release of *Thank Me Later* (2010), interview with Brad Wete, Entertainment Weekly, December 19, 2019.

It gets lonely two times for me: one, when I see people's normal lives progressing, like falling in love, marriage, getting a job. When I catch glimpses of the life that I could have had – not that I'd ever want to go back – but it does make you feel a bit like, 'Damn, I hope this is the right path and I hope I'm going to be OK.'

Drake, on questioning whether his life's path was the right one, interview with Damien Scott, *Complex*, November 15, 2011.

Drake has 13 No.1 U.S. hits on the Billboard Hot 100, a joint-record for the most No.1 singles by a male solo artist.

The record is tied with none other than... Michael Jackson!

We may be worlds apart in the sense of where you're from, where I'm from, what I'm doing, what you're doing, but I'm only ever rapping about very simple human emotions: love, triumph, failure, nerves, fear, doubt. It doesn't matter what you're doing – you gotta at least hear what I'm saying to you. And I pray that it helps. When I make an album, all I want you to know is I hear you.

Drake, on what he hopes his fans hear in his music, interview with Leon Neyfakh, *Fader*, September 24, 2015.

The thing that I'm the most proud of is that I was able to earn money at a very important time in my life and give my mother more years on her life, because she needed a very expensive surgery on her spine. I don't know if we would have been able to get the same doctor and the same treatment had I not worked hard enough to make that money. So, that is what I'm most proud of, that my mother is here and she's healthier than ever and taking vacations and smiling.

Drake, on his proudest achievement to date, interview with Milly McMahon, *i-D*, October 2012.

"

I wish that we lived in a time and a generation where people would stop viewing my honesty as overly emotional. People always act like I spend my life crying in a dark room. I don't. I'm a man.

"

Drake, on his "sensitive" reputation, interview with Mark Anthony Green, *GQ*, November 11, 2011.

One of my goals in life is to have the biggest residential pool on the planet. An Olympic-size pool inside the house.

Drake, on his greatest ambition, interview with Jonah Weiner, *Rolling Stone*, February 13, 2014.

"

Don't fuck with me.

"

Drake, on his beefs with artists such as Kendrick Lamar and Kanye West, interview with Elliot Wilson, *Respect*, September 13, 2019.

“Those were harsh words, right? It’s like, you can’t just say that and then see me and pretend like nothing ever happened. That’s not real, man.”

Drake, on Kendrick Lamar name-checking Drake in 'Not Like Us', reigniting their now-infamous beef which began in 2013, interview with Sam Wolfson, *NME*, April 13, 2016.

“

We were probably the only family that had four thesauruses in the house. I’d tell Aubrey, ‘When you’re expressing yourself, try and find other words you can use.’

”

Sandi Graham, Drake’s mom,* on his love of rhyming and language at an early age, interview with Jonah Weiner, *Rolling Stone*, February 13, 2014

*One day, when Drake was about 10, Sandi entered his bedroom and saw a vision of the future: Drake was standing on the mattress, pretending that a toilet-paper roll was a microphone, rapping lyrics he’d written.

In 2021, *The Guardian* ranked Drake's top 10 most essential tracks.

Do you agree?

1. 'Nice For What'
2. 'Child's Play'
3. 'Hold On, We're Going Home'
4. 'Hotline Bling'
5. 'Portland'
6. 'Know Yourself'
7. 'Laugh Now Cry Later'
8. 'Started From the Bottom'
9. 'Fancy'
10. 'The Ride'

I never really thought I was that big of a deal because there were kids around me whose lights seemed to be shining much brighter than mine.

Drake, on his first taste of local fame during his tenure on the teen soap drama *Degrassi: The Next Generation*, interview with Sam Wolfson, *NME*, April 13, 2016.

Timeless.

”

Drake, when asked ‘One word that describes you is?’, interview with Leslie Woods, *WRG Magazine*, 2006.

I know good and well that Kendrick's not murdering me, at all, in any platform. So when that day presents itself, I guess we can revisit the topic.

Drake, on his beef with Kendrick Lamar, interview with *Billboard*, September 7, 2013.

I'm a realist. It's not like I'm thinking my debut album is going sell a million copies in a week.*

”

Drake, on his debut album 2010's *Thank Me Later*, interview with Shanel Obum, *Vibe*, February 26, 2009.

*It did.

I'm not overwhelmed by what everyone else wants this first album to be – I'm overwhelmed by what I know I need it to be.

Drake, on the colossal expectation of his debut album, 2010's *Thank Me Later*, interview with Dimitri Ehrlich, *Interview*, December 2, 2009.

I swear I'm not sitting around going, 'What's the new meme going to be?' I'm trying to make anthems that are empowering to people and to find phrases that I haven't heard before.

”

Drake, on his supreme viral meme-worthiness, interview with *Billboard*, September 7, 2013.

There's these memes about me, these stupid stereotypes people have of me as this overly emotional character that cries in his room every night. There are jokes because of *Degrassi*, because I'm Canadian, because I make music for women. There are memes of guys crying to my music. I love it. I heart those photos when I see them on Instagram.

Drake, on the millions of social media viral memes he inspires, interview with Jonah Weiner, *Rolling Stone*, February 13, 2014.

I've got crazy family history – my grandmother used to baby-sit for Aretha Franklin.

”

Drake, on his family's connections to musical superstars, interview with Jonah Weiner, *Rolling Stone*, February 13, 2014.

Lil Wayne was high out of his mind, getting these big wings tattooed on his body on the tour bus, for like six straight hours. And out of nowhere, everyone got on the bus and the bus started moving. I just kept my mouth shut. Rolled for like a week, ended up in Atlanta.

”

Drake, on the first time he met Lil Wayne, and his life changed forever, interview with Amos Barshad, *Heeb*, June 18, 2010.

CHAPTER THREE

TEAM DRIZZY

Drake is known as a feast of memorable nicknames, from 6 God to The Boy, Heartbreak Drake to Wheelchair Jimmy, Champagne Papi to October's Very Own, but to his most loyal fans Drake is is best known as Drizzy.

That's why they call themselves Team Drizzy. Wanna join?

“

Yes, I wear sweaters!
No, I don’t give a fuck!

”

Drake, on his iconic sweater-wearing that breaks the Internet regularly, interview with Ajon Brodie, *Fader*, September 23, 2013.

My father gave me my full name – Aubrey Drake Graham. His reasoning behind it, I am not sure. My dad is a character so it could be anything. I just really loved the name and I embraced it my whole life. I use Aubrey more for the acting, which is how I separate myself. I like the fact that I have two names because I find that in this industry you have to have dual personalities, especially being an actor going into music. Drake is me in my everyday life, Drake is who I am and Aubrey is more of a separate, sort of 'proper' individual.

Drake, on the origins of his birth name, and his reason to use his middle name Drake as his stage name, interview with *HipHopCanada*, July 12, 2006.

You know the way fighters don't fuck before the fight? Sometimes I feel like I'm so focused on training my body and getting my mind right to create this album that sex isn't one of my main priorities.

Drake, on staying focused despite distractions, interview with Michael Paterniti, *GQ*, June 18, 2013.

“

With acting you’re dependent on so much stuff that you don’t control. I don’t like that. With music, I go to the studio, I record the song, if it works it works, if it doesn’t it doesn’t. That’s how music is and I like that formula way better.

”

Drake, on why he’s not currently pursuing his acting career, interview with Milly McMahon, *the i-D*, October 2012.

I make music that may cause kids to actually think.

Drake, on the potential of his music, interview with Leslie Woods, *WRG Magazine*, 2006.

“

I don’t do the dumb shit to get in trouble. If I’m drunk I’m gonna go out the back door. I ain’t gonna walk out the front so you see me stumbling and dropping my keys. I’m not that guy, I’m not that dumb. I wanna be in this position as long as I possibly can. Any sex tape I’ve ever made… I own it.

”

Drake, on keeping clear of controversies and scandals, interview with Sam Wolfson, *NME*, April 13, 2016.

I want to prove that there's distance between me and the people considered to be my peers. I have something special.

”

Drake, on being different to his rap contemporaries, such as A$AP Rocky and Kendrick Lamar, interview with Jonah Weiner, *Rolling Stone*, February 13, 2014.

I want to be remembered as an artist that gave you a piece of me, as opposed to some surface bullshit. I don't think people realize that we die, we leave here, and either they forget about you or remember you. And how they remember you is up to you. I just want to be remembered as a poet that was open and honest because I wake up every morning and I'm me.

”

Drake, on what he hopes to be remembered for, interview with Mark Anthony Green, *GQ*, November 11, 2011.

“

Early on, around the first album, I used to have this mentality where I’d be at the Grammys or at the MTV awards, sitting at my seat, thinking, ‘Oh, God, I hope they cancel my performance’ – I was that nervous. But now I’m just like, ‘Man, I hope they give me five extra minutes.’

”

Drake, on his increasing self-confidence and love of performing live, interview with Jonah Weiner, *Rolling Stone*, February 13, 2014.

It would have to be Jay-Z's 'Lucky Me', which would then fade into Marvin Gaye's 'T Plays it Cool', which would progress into T.I.'s 'I Can't Quit', and then end off with the melodic sounds of George Benson's 'Affirmation'. I can't pick one so it has to be a medley.

”

Drake, when asked ,"If you had to pick one song to be the soundtrack of your life, what would it be and why?", interview with Leslie Woods, *WRG Magazine*, 2006.

Everybody thinks I went to some private school and my family was rich. Maybe it's my fault. Maybe I haven't talked enough about it, but I didn't grow up happy. I wasn't in a happy home. My mother was very sick.

Drake, on his unhappy home life during his teenage years, interview with Damien Scott, *Complex*, November 15, 2011.

February 9, 2025

While Drake's No.1 enemy Kendrick Lamar was performing his headline-grabbing Drake diss-track 'Not Like Us' at the now-infamous Superbowl Halftime Show 2025, Drake was the *other* side of the world in Melbourne, Australia, performing live at the Rod Laver Arena to 35,000 fans.

Drake played 41 songs, with an encore of 'IDGAF', 'Rich Flex' and 'Yebba's Heartbreak'.

Curiosity is the best part of working with any kind of artist. You want to see how somebody else's process works. It's like learning a secret. My mother was a teacher, and she brought all kinds of things into our house. So I learned early on that inspiration could come in many forms, from many people.

”

Drake, on his famous collaborations with a wealth of iconic pop, rock, rap and hip-hop artists, interview with Lynn Hirschberg, *W Magazine*, October 15, 2015.

I'm really trying. It's not like I'm just sitting here, just fuckin' shooting with my eyes closed. I'm really trying to make music for your life.

Drake, on his passion for making music that connects deeply with an audience, interview with Leon Neyfakh, *Fader*, September 24, 2015.

Hell must feel like how Toronto feels on any given winter day, and winter lasts seven months. It's my favourite place in the world, but there's this cold, gloomy, dark vibe. It produces a certain sound.

Drake, on his love of his hometown, interview with Jonah Weiner, *Rolling Stone*, February 13, 2014.

My whole life is about chasing what's next, so, we're sitting here talking about *Take Care* and how successful it is, but I couldn't care less because I have another album to make and I don't want to relish in my own success. I think about the next thing.

"

Drake, on his need to constantly keep moving, interview with Milly McMahon, *i-D*, October 2012.

Whether it's in your headphones at the gym, or your car, I just want you to have that experience before you read online how this beat sounds or read someone's opinion on what the worst song on the album is. Reviews condition people. I just want people to be able to form their own opinion.

Drake, on his decision to no longer do press interviews ahead of album releases, interview with Brad Wete, Entertainment Weekly, December 19, 2019.

I push myself in a lot of aspects when I write a song. I write a piece and where most people would stop and say, 'Oh, that's the hook right there,' I'll move that to the first four bars of the verse and do a new hook. That's how I like to challenge myself. I'll write something and everyone that's around might be like, 'Oh that's that hook right there.' And then I'll write something even better than that.

Drake, on the "Drake Formula" to writing instant hits, interview with Brad Wete, Entertainment Weekly, December 19, 2019.

I've seen a lot. I've seen a lot of life. I've been with the most blessed kids in the world. I've been with people whose life is right at the bottom of the barrel. I was on a TV show, I went to art school, I went to hood schools. I've lived.

Drake, on the variety of life he's experienced at the age of 24, interview with Damien Scott, *Complex*, November 15, 2011.

"

For a lot of music fans, albums are time markers. *So Far Gone* is a time marker. You may have had a different girlfriend at that time or not graduated for school yet. Life may have been simpler. So when people say, 'They miss the old Drake', I just think they're saying they miss that time in their lives. Great. They associate me with that time in their life. But any real fan would want me to evolve and get better. I can't go back to the old me. It's impossible. I'm proud of who I've evolved into.

"

Drake, on evolving his sound with each new album or mixtape, interview with Brad Wete, Entertainment Weekly, December 19, 2019.

Drake holds an impressive collection of Guinness World Records, including:

– most streams on Spotify in one year for a male musician

– most streamed act on Spotify

– most simultaneous new entries in the Hot 100 by a solo act

– most streams for tracks from one album in a week

– most Billboard music awards won by an artist in a single year

– most consecutive weeks in Top 10 of U.S. Hot 100 (male)

– most streamed album on Apple Music in 24 hours

– the biggest-selling digital artist in the U.S.

Sometimes I will sit on a song for a minute because I will wait to experience something that inspires me.

Drake, on his earliest songwriting processes, interview with Leslie Woods, *WRG Magazine*, 2006.

"For the first time ever. One artist. Three different setlists."

In 2025 Drake became the first artist ever to headline all three nights of London's Wireless festival to celebrate the prestigious festival's 20th anniversary.

Each night Drake played a different set, from Friday July 11 to Sunday July 13, to more than 150,000 fans in total. The Wireless performance was Drake's first UK gig since he last performed at Wireless in 2021 with co-headliner Nicki Minaj.

To celebrate this momentous occasion, Wireless announced that "Drake holds the title for the Wireless's audience's most requested artist".

I'm not worried about these other rappers, I'm not competing with those guys. I already know their hand, I know their move. I'm worried about the kid that's sitting in his house that wants to be better than me and all those guys. That's who I'm competing with.

Drake, on the next generation of rappers and hip-hop artists, interview with Alexander Iadarola, *Fader*, June 24, 2015.

At Drake's bar mitzvah in 1999, aged 13, the rapper requested the Backstreet Boys' 1998 hit 'I Want It That Way' as his song of the night.

The song has remained one of Drake's favourites. He even performed it live in Toronto, Canada, with the Backstreet Boys in 2022, stating:

"At my bar mitzvah, for the first time in my life, this girl that I was in love with came up to me while one of the greatest songs in the world was playing… and she asked me if I would dance with her. It was the first time I ever felt acknowledged. It was the first time I ever felt like I had a shot at being cool."

Hip-hop isn't not being famous. Hip-hop isn't struggling. Hip-hop is music! It's a sound, a feeling, an emotion. It's not about where you're at in your career. I'm proud of what I'm doing in the mainstream. I wouldn't do it any different. All the things about life I want to say, I say. And they play my songs on the radio.

”

Drake, on being considered too mainstream to be an honest hip-hop artist, interview with Chris Lee, *Los Angeles Times*, June 14, 2010.

I know everything. I know everything that's being said about you. I know everything that's being said about me. I'm very in tune with this life.

”

Drake, on being "in tune" with his status and life, interview with Leon Neyfakh, *Fader*, September 24, 2015.

Beef with Kendrick

In February 2025 Kendrick Lamar, Drake's rap nemesis, reignited his decade-long feud with Drake in the most spectacular fashion – during the Super Bowl LIX at the Caesars Superdome in New Orleans, Louisiana. During the 13-minute halftime set, Lamar used his 2024 Drake diss-tracks 'Not Like Us', 'Meet the Grahams' and 'Euphoria' to fling serious allegations at Drake.

The rapper responded by suing Lamar's label, Universal Music Group (UMG), for defamation and harassment.

What happens next is anyone's guess.

CHAPTER
FOUR

YOLO

Over the years, Drake has become synonymous with a selection of superfly swag, from having the greatest (and largest!) sweater collection in pop to flying around in a custom-built private jet so luxurious he had to named it after himself – Air Drake.*

He's also famous for living true to his motto: you only live once. For proof, turn the page…

*The sky-blue Boeing 767 famously has 'If you're reading this, we left' printed on its undercarriage. Iconic.

“

No. But I’m working on it.

”

Drake, when asked ‘Do you see yourself as a sex symbol?’, interview with Damien Scott, *Complex*, November 15, 2011.

I remember when artists used to take four years to make an album. Usher used to disappear for three years. It took Justin Timberlake a really long time to craft *Justified*. Even Beyoncé's albums are spanned three years apart. You've got to live, man. And now we've sort of birthed and encouraged this generation of instant gratification.

Drake, on the importance of taking time out to live in between album releases, interview with Brad Wete, Entertainment Weekly, December 19, 2019.

"

From *So Far Gone* to *Thank Me Later* to *Take Care*, I'm starting to develop a 'Drake Formula' for songs.

"

Drake, on the "Drake Formula", interview with Thomas Golianopoulos, *XXL*, August 28, 2013.

I want to set the bar so high for myself. I don't want to do it like everyone else. I want to make original songs and call it a mixtape. When I write I like to just say everything that people think about but never express vocally. I just get deep into it; I'm a bit obsessive about music.

”

Drake, on his first mixtape, 2006's *Room For Improvement*, interview with *HipHopCanada*, July 12, 2006.

I pull my weight when it comes to my pen. Anybody that knows me knows that my strongest talent is writing. That's why people ask me to write songs for them.

Drake, on his passion and reputation for writing songs, interview with Elliott Wilson, Rap Radar podcast, December 26, 2019.

My music has always belonged to the people.

Drake, on being a man, and voice, of the people, interview with Gerrick D Kennedy, *Los Angeles Times*, November 8, 2011.

I guess my only concern is: will my life evolve enough that my story remains interesting?

”

Drake, on wanting to remain relevant and interesting to his fans, interview with John Crossingham, *Men's Fashion*, Autumn 2010.

I'm the captain of a ship, and I look behind me and I see a lot of people on board. Full steam ahead. That's just how I have to keep rocking for right now. Hopefully I can find somebody that can just stand beside me at the wheel and help me steer while we keep the journey going as opposed to me having to pull over because that person is getting seasick.

Drake, on the possibility of maybe one day getting married, interview with Elliott Wilson, Rap Radar podcast, December 26, 2019.

I just want to be remembered as somebody who was himself. Not a product.

”

Drake, on his legacy, interview with Leon Neyfakh, *Fader*, September 24, 2015.

I really hope that there's fans who sit with the music and drive to it and just really soak it in – not just run back to the computer and demand more. It's important for our generation to know that it's okay to take some time. It's okay if an album takes a year or two to make. That just means it's probably going to be better than if they took two months and released it.

Drake, on the importance of taking time to make – and listen to, and appreciate – new music, interview with Brad Wete, Entertainment Weekly, December 19, 2019.

King of Toronto? First of all I never self-proclaimed myself as that, period. But I'll take it.

99

Drake, on being referred to in the press as the "King of Toronto" following his rapid rise to success, interview with Damien Scott, *Complex*, November 15, 2011.

I'm a young man of substance. I don't want to waste time chasing empty connections.

Drake, on time-wasting, interview with Robert Everett Green, *Globe and Mail*, December 18, 2009.

I'm a vessel to deliver emotion to people. I want to provide the background music to your life as you live it. I'm there for you in heartbreak and tragedy and joy. The thought of being remembered is what keeps me going. The negatives don't matter – it's history that counts.

”

Drake, on his aspirations for his music long-term, interview with Lynn Hirschberg, *W Magazine*, October 15, 2015.

The Internet has fucked the game up so bad that if I don't do it, I'm curious to sit back and watch whoever does. If *Thank Me Later* doesn't do what I think it's gonna do, I'm very curious to see the next artist, birthed in this Internet generation, that will go on to sell millions of records.

Drake, on his debut album, 2010's *Thank Me Later*, and how the rap landscape has changed in the Internet age, interview with Amos Barshad, *Heeb*, June 18, 2010.

I was in so much trouble with the producers. I had like three and a half strikes against my name.

”

Drake, on getting in trouble with the *Degrassi* TV producers for focusing on his music too much, interview with Amos Barshad, *Heeb*, June 18, 2010.

“

I went to a Jewish school, where nobody understood what it was like to be black and Jewish. The same kids that made fun of me then are super proud of me now. And they act as if nothing happened.

”

Drake, on growing up bi-racial and Jewish, interview with Amos Barshad, *Heeb*, June 18, 2010.

I've made very smart, conscious decisions that have landed me here. I can't attribute that to money or fame. That's just attributed to the way I treat people.

”

Drake, on using his fame for good and being a nice guy along the way, interview with Damien Scott, *Complex*, November 15, 2011.

I won't even rap on a beat unless it's got some magic element of new tempo or new pocket, where I hear myself and feel like I've stumbled upon something new.

”

Drake, on his desire to discover something new with his sound, interview with Leon Neyfakh, *Fader*, September 24, 2015.

“

There are a lot of eyes on me, a lot of pressure on me. And I just want to be someone people remember. I want to speak for this generation.

Drake, on the pressures of being called the "world's most successful musician", interview with Brad Wete, Entertainment Weekly, December 19, 2019.

I really want to turn the club upside down. But I want to do it with integrity – with soul.

”

Drake, on being popular but not at the sake of being a mere product, interview with Sam Wolfson, *NME*, April 13, 2016.

I don't write lyrics down on paper. The other day, I was in the studio with Alicia Keys, and I wrote two songs just speaking to her. I wish I could write that way for rap. With my rap songs, there's so much of me I have to give that I don't know if I could ever just flow.

”

Drake, on writing songs for R&B and its difference to writing songs for rap, interview with *Complex*, January 25, 2010.

February 14, 2025

The day Drake released his collaborative studio album *$ome $exy $ongs 4 U*, produced with Canadian singer PartyNextDoor.

The album's release day on Valentine's Day is no accident – Drake's third album released on the special day – and at 21 tracks and 73 minutes, *$ome $exy $ongs 4 U* is the "perfect soundtrack length" for lovers looking to Netflix & Chill!

I write best about two things: the constant quest to have, and understand, love and money.

”

Drake, on his two main lyrical themes, interview with *Complex*, January 25, 2010.

I have always sort of been alone in my world. I've never really been connected to anything. I don't think I ever want to find my place.

”

Drake, on sensing his own isolation from the world, interview with Edward Houghton, *Fader*, September 1, 2009.

I fell for somebody I liked so much. Not a celebrity, just a normal girl. She was like, 'I won't be in a relationship with you, you're a rapper and I think more of myself than go through the bullshit.' That killed me.

Drake, on fame and success impacting his personal life, interview with Sam Wolfson, *NME*, April 13, 2016.

If I didn't have it together I wouldn't be able to be that open and honest with you. I think that people think my life is just a shambles and it's really not. The reason I can make an album like *Views* is because I actually have a grip on my life. I recognise all my issues.

Drake, on his 2016 album Views, a highly personal record, interview with Sam Wolfson, *NME*, April 13, 2016.

By the Numbers

Since his arrival in 2010, Drake has become the world's most iconic solo artist, breaking records and smashing huge sales and streaming records…

- More than 110 billion total streams on Spotify* (February 2025)
- More than 12.5 billion total views on YouTube (February 2025)
- More than 244 million digital singles sold worldwide
- More than 170 million albums sold worldwide

* Drake is the most-streamed male artist in Spotify's history!

- More than 145 million followers on Instagram
- More than 75 million monthly listeners on Spotify (February 2025)
- Ranked the 16th Greatest Artist of All Time by Billboard
- Won more than 200 awards, including five Grammy Awards, 39 Billboard Music Awards, and six American Music Award
- More than 13 No.1 singles in the U.S. Billboard Charts
- Drake's fourth album, *Views*, has sold more than 10 million copies!

CHAPTER FIVE

CHAMPAGNE PAPI

To his 145+ million Instagram followers, Drake is known as Champagne Papi, the rich babby daddy that lives a life of luxury. But Drake isn't beloved by all.

He's forever squashing beefs, fending off feuds and fighting his own inner demons. As he says himself: "Life is never all good. I live by that."

At this point, I can't have anybody but 40. Sometimes you'll hear me screaming halfway across the house – '40! 40!' It's the euphoric feeling of having completed something and I'm ready to record it now.

Drake, on Noah "40" Shebib, his music producer and partner, interview with Michael Paterniti, *GQ*, June 18, 2013.

I was in class, and I used to always crack jokes in class. I was a good liar and a good talker. And this kid in my class was like, 'Yo, my dad is an agent. You should go talk to him because you make people laugh.' I was my father's son. I was slick, you know? When it comes to knowing what to say, to charm, I always had it.

Drake, on how he secured a talent agent aged 14, interview with Claire Hoffman, *GQ*, April 13, 2012.

When my mother was getting surgery I went on Twitter, something I rarely do, and I tweeted, I don't know why, 'Give praise to my mom today'. And I got a response like, 'I hope your mom dies in surgery'. I was like, Wow, what a disconnected world we are a part of. I've heard it all.

”

Drake, on the evils of being famous in the age of social media, interview with Damien Scott, *Complex*, November 15, 2011.

I didn't say I was the rap Hendrix or Marley. I said I was the descendant. Because I feel like that's what I want to be for this generation: iconic. That's the purpose I want to serve on this earth. I want my words to be remembered.

”

Drake, on creating an enduring legacy, interview with Paul Lester, *The Guardian*, March 29, 2012.

I came up from underneath the stage and it looked like I was looking at the sky and all the lights flashing were stars. It was as clear as day. I saw all these lights and thought, Wow this is it, this is my time.

Drake, on his sold-out show at London's O2 (one of only four rappers ever to sell out the arena), interview with Milly McMahon, *i-D*, October 2012.

“

Rap about my life. Often, people are like, whoa, are you really gonna say that?

Drake, when asked to describe the most fearless thing he'd done, interview with Ina Azodi, *Cosmopolitan*, March 7, 2011.

"

Do I make music you enjoy? Fine. What does it matter where I came from?

"

Drake, on feeling he has to prove himself to his haters about the authenticity of his origins, interview with Damien Scott, *Complex*, November 15, 2011.

I've been around a lot of shit in my life. I just don't solicit those stories. I don't brag about my hood stories. But I've done a lot for the streets.

Drake, on being ridiculed for claiming he's "from the hood", interview with Damien Scott, *Complex*, November 15, 2011.

I don't have a diary, so I use my music as time markers. *So Far Gone* is still as powerful as ever to me because it allows me to vividly remember where I was at that time and because I talk about such personal things. It almost is a reminder to myself of who I was dating at that time and what I was driving. I'm very precise about the things that I talk about and therefore my music doesn't lose its value to me.

”

Drake, on music as memories, interview with Amanda Dobbins, *Vulture*, November 14, 2011.

To date, Drake has released eight studio albums and seven mixtapes as a solo artist, as well as countless other collaborations.

Which one is your favourite?

1. *Thank Me Later* (2010)
2. *Take Care* (2011)
3. *Nothing Was the Same* (2013)
4. *Views* (2016)
5. *Scorpion* (2018)
6. *Certified Lover Boy* (2021)
7. *Honestly, Nevermind* (2022)
8. *For All the Dogs* (2023)

The seconds after a man reaches climax, that's like the realest moment of your life. If I don't want you next to me in the next twenty seconds, then there's something wrong.

”

Drake, on the obstacles he faces regarding the bountiful supply of sex he receives as a famous musician, interview with Claire Hoffman, *GQ*, April 13, 2012.

I don't want to go brag about having it all. 'Oh, I just got the new crib with the pool' – cause it just sounds stupid. But if fans were to come my house, they'd be like, 'Oh, shit. Okay, I get it. You're a kid from Toronto and now you live here. This *is* fucked up.'

99

Drake, on his life being "fucked up" relative to a fans' perspective, interview with Claire Hoffman, *GQ*, April 13, 2012.

The Year of Drake

If 2013 (infamously) belonged to Miley Cyrus, then 2015 famously belonged to Drake.

The year saw Drake break out with two stunning mixtapes, *If You're Reading This It's Too Late* and *What A Time To Be Alive* – becoming the first hip-hop artist since 2004 to have two No. 1 projects in the same year – as well as the massive global-hit single 'Hotline Bling', which sold more than two million copies in the U.S. alone.

'Take Care' is a phrase I use in passing conversation to dismiss bullshit like, 'Oh, you couldn't make it on time? Oh, take care, take care.' We've always used that and then I really took so much care making this album. I knew I was going to go home and take longer than six months, I knew that I was literally going to take care of making this project and be attentive, be clear, be immersed in it, so the title 'Take Care' worked.

99

Drake, on the purpose behind 2011's *Take Care*, and its title, interview with Sam Wolfson, *NME*, April 13, 2016.

The point is, the sweaters* meme thing is a result of the fact that I don't give people enough to talk about as far as my life goes. They need something to nitpick at.

”

Drake, on his sweater-wearing as a global phenomenon, interview with Amanda Dobbins, *Vulture*, November 14, 2011

* Drake owns more than 400 sweaters. "I don't ever do a zip-up. I'm a pullover guy," he once claimed.

At the 2017 Billboard Music Awards Drake won 13 awards, breaking the record for the most wins in a single night, largely due to the phenomenal stateside success of 2016 album *Views*.

Accepting the award, Drake ended his beefs with Ludacris and Nicki Minaj and thanked mentor Lil Wayne. "If it wasn't for the risks you took, none of us would be here tonight," Drake said.

When my dad drove me to Memphis one time from Toronto, a 20-hour drive, I brought my *Doggystyle* [Snoop Doggy Dogg] cassette. I asked him, 'Dad, can I please play this?' He was like, 'Yeah. You can play it for 20 minutes.' And then we listened to an hour of my music.

Drake, on a precious formative memory of the importance of music, interview with Claire Hoffman, *GQ*, April 13, 2012.

It's never all good. I live by that saying. That's how I protect myself in life.

Drake, on his life motto, interview with Sam Wolfson, *NME*, April 13, 2016.

When I finish writing a rap verse, it's a lot like sex: you start off slow with ideas, like foreplay, and then you put your all into it. When you end it with the perfect thought, it's like that perfect last stroke.

”

Drake, on rap music and sex, interview with Ina Azodi, *Cosmopolitan*, March 7, 2011.

I've put myself in a position where nobody can tell me what kind of songs to do or how many to put on the album. There are no restrictions. I don't care about anybody's voice outside of my fans'. I'm never going to play things safe. I just want people to have great music. Music got me through a lot of shit. I just want to give people enough to where they're satisfied.

Drake, on Team Drizzy and forever taking musical risks for the sake of his fans, interview with Brad Wete, Entertainment Weekly, December 19, 2019.

I want to service people through fall, winter, spring and into the next summer. I want this music to last. I want to create something that has a long shelf life than the average album these days.

”

Drake, on creating and releasing music that endures, interview with Brad Wete, Entertainment Weekly, December 19, 2019.

YOLO

In 2011 Drake's track 'The Motto', the fourth single from his second studio album *Take Care* (2011), was released, featuring Lil Wayne.

The song sold more than three million singles and is credited with popularizing the acronym "YOLO" (You Only Live Once) worldwide.

It was shortlisted by the Oxford American Dictionary as Word of the Year, though it was beaten to the top spot by "GIF".

February 13, 2009

The day Drake's life changed forever. He dropped his third mixtape: *So Far Gone*. It was instantly considered a commercial smash and made Drake a household name.

"The title has a lot of meanings: as the way we carry ourselves, the way we dress, the way people view us. Not to sound cocky, it's just that feeling that we're just distanced in a good way," Drake told *Complex* in 2009. "You're just elevating past the bullshit and past all the shit that you used to be a part of and you're not that proud of, you're just so far gone."

I don't really have a gimmick or a 'thing'. I'm one of the few artists who gets to be himself every day. It doesn't take me six hours to get ready, and I don't have to wake up in the morning and remember to act like this or talk like that. I just have to be me. And people really like that.

Drake, on being true to himself, interview with Jenny Stevens, *NME*, July 27, 2012.

May 21, 2021

The day Drake was awarded the highly prestigious "Artist of the Decade" award at the 2021 Billboard Music Awards.

During the 2010s, Drake banked nine No.1s and smashed pretty much every U.S. music record. Accepting the award he said, "I know I've spent an incalculable amount of hours trying to analyse all the things that I've done wrong. But tonight for once, I'm sure as hell I did something right."

"I'm obsessed with perfection. I want to work. I don't want to take this for granted. But perfection for me is not a visual image of perfection. Perfection to me is working as hard as I possibly can at 100 per cent. That's perfection."

Drake, on his definition of perfection, interview with Claire Hoffman, *GQ*, April 13, 2012.

I want to move through life in the most non-confrontational way possible, but I'm not a pussy. Don't ever get that mixed up.

Drake, on being a pacificist (not a pussy) when it comes to squashing beefs, interview with Damien Scott, *Complex*, November 15, 2011.

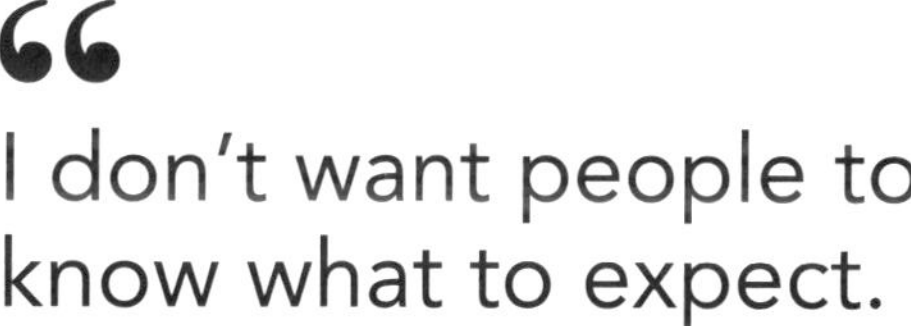

Drake, on *Take Care*, interview with Brad Wete, Entertainment Weekly, December 19, 2019.

CHAPTER SIX

LAST NAME: EVER. FIRST NAME: GREATEST

In 2009 – before he even released his debut album! – Drake proved himself a worthy heir to the rap throne when he appeared with Kanye West, Eminem and Lil Wayne with his killer verse on the track 'Forever'.

There, he made his declaration of intent as clear as day when he famously rapped, "Last name: Ever. First name: Greatest."

An icon was born...

There have been times when a negative comment about me would be the be all and end all, and I'd wonder, why do you hate me so much? Artists are only human, and we seek validation like everyone else.

Drake, on his haters and his critics, interview with Paul Lester, *The Guardian*, March 29, 2012.

When I was in my mom's house, I had nowhere to go, no real obligations, I didn't have anything else. And that made for some of the best music I've made. Records where I felt small. That feeling is hard to capture when you're sitting out here in a space with a pool, a tennis court, a volleyball court and a stables. It's really difficult for me to find something that makes me feel small.

”

Drake, on fame and fortune as creative obstacles, interview with Claire Hoffman, *GQ*, April 13, 2012.

November 4, 2001

The day Drake made his debut acting performance in the third episode ('Family Politics') of season one of *Degrassi: The Next Generation* as popular jock Jimmy Brooks. Drake starred in seven seasons and more than 100 episodes from 2001 to 2008.

Throughout the show much happens to Jimmy Brooks, including rapping his very first rhyme (called 'Tell Me Lies') and, in Season Four episode 'Time Stands Still', Jimmy was paralyzed after a school shooting.

In 2017, Drake tweeted that he still gets annual residuals from his seven years on *Degrassi*, posting a photo of a check for... $8.25

I'm not soft. I'm just not one of those people who's closed off emotionally. I went through too much with my father and my mother, watching her go through her shit and be hurt... I've seen too many people cry.

”

Drake, on his oft-ridiculed reputation for being "soft" and "sensitive", interview with Paul Lester, *The Guardian*, March 29, 2012.

It was all white Jewish kids, and it was tough. I didn't have the worst time, but I did have a hard time. I was always the last kid to get the invite to the party.

”

Drake, on being an outcast at Forest Hill Collegiate Institute, his public high school, interview with Jonah Weiner, *Rolling Stone*, February 13, 2014.

I don't know how long I necessarily want to make rap music for. There are artists that are 35 and upwards who still make rap and it still works for them. I don't know if I'll be that guy.

”

Drake, on whether he'll still rapping past 35, interview with Milly McMahon, *i-D*, October 2012.

“

When you’re on the road and moving city to city, when someone isn’t there at the end of the night, you feel empty. There was a point where I felt like I needed to keep the company of a different woman every night. I used to be filling a void. And if you happen to be with somebody that isn’t someone you want to converse with, you start feeling like, I wish I was just here watching *True Blood* by myself.

”

Drake, on the perils of his earliest fame, interview with Mickey Rapkin, *Elle*, October 13, 2011.

I never use my outlet for confrontation or negativity, ever. I always just try to give people music to ride to and music to enjoy. All I ever ask in return is that it's mutual love. That's it.

Drake, on wanting to be a positive influence, interview with Damien Scott, *Complex*, November 15, 2011.

"I promise you, I already won."

In 2019, while accepting the Grammy Award for Best Rap Song for 'God's Plan', Drake's speech was cut off as he was about to bash the Grammys, a ceremony Drake has long considered out-of-touch with the rap community.

He said: "This is a business where sometimes it's up to a bunch of people who might not understand what a mixed-race kid from Canada has to say, but if you have people who are singing your songs word for word, if you are a hero in your hometown, if there are people who have regular jobs who are coming out in the rain, in the snow, spending their hard-earned money to buy tickets to come to your shows, you've already won, you don't need this right here."

Drake won his first Grammy in 2013 for Best Rap Album for *Take Care*.

If I wasn't a rapper, and I was back home in Toronto, and I had my job that kept me in the city, my girl would be my life. I have a lot of friends back there, and their relationships have become the focal point, the high point of their lives. And that's cool. I just have new goals, new places to go, new people to meet. I live off a different high point every day.

”

Drake, on life back home in Toronto, interview with Michael Paterniti, *GQ*, June 18, 2013.

“

My dad was messing up pretty bad for drug-related stuff and theft. He was a mover and a shaker – a hustler. If you had it, he could sell it for you.

”

Drake, on his father and their relationship, interview with Jonah Weiner, *Rolling Stone*, February 13, 2014.

Rihanna was the first girl with any fame that paid me any mind. You spend days reading about this person in the magazines. All of a sudden you have this No.1 song and you're at some birthday party and there she is. And you're just some naive kid from Toronto staying in some shitty-ass hotel who got invited to this party on a whim. That's just how it happened.

Drake, on his on-off relationship with Rihanna during the 2010s, interview with Mickey Rapkin, *Elle*, October 13, 2011.

I'm not sure what I mean to this generation; I won't understand until my story plays out. But there is that vision of the legacy. There's also so many opportunities to plummet and not reach that. But I keep pushing forward. There are only two directions you can go.

Drake, on striving to keep looking forward with his work, interview with John Kennedy, *Vibe*, December 30, 2013.

“I'm living the truth. I wake up in the morning and my heart is light, man. It's not heavy. I don't have skeletons in the closet on their way out. This is my real age, my real name, my real past, and I'm good with that.”

Drake, on living a truthful life, interview with Michael Paterniti, *GQ*, June 18, 2013.

What did we just do? Did we shift the needle on the culture, or did we just sort of potentially bomb any hope of being respected as a real rapper?

”

Drake, on his risk-taking 2009 remix of Lykke Li's 'Little Bit', interview with Thomas Golianopoulos, *XXL*, August 28, 2013.

I was always this kid looking from the outside into this world that I call 'Houstatlantavegas', which is just any given city at any given point in the night time filed with beautiful women, money, evils and darkness. I was always intrigued by the nightlife.

Drake, on the lyrical theme of 2010's *Thank Me Later*, interview with Damien Scott, *Complex*, November 15, 2011.

“

With So Far Gone, we were so deeply immersed in the sound that we had created we didn’t know if we had created the most beautiful balance in the world, or if we were out of our minds. To get back there mentally, it’s what I’m trying to do right now – that feeling, like you’re standing on a cliff and closing your eyes and saying, ‘Fuck it.’

”

Drake, on his pioneering and innovative third mixtape, 2009’s *So Far Gone*, interview with Amos Barshad, *Heeb*, June 18, 2010.

I fully accept I'm an arena-touring act. When I'm writing, I'm thinking about how the songs are going to play live. Fifty bars of rap don't translate onstage. No matter how potent the music, you lose the crowd. They want a hook; they want to sing your stuff back to you. That's why on this album I've been trying to condense my thoughts to sixteen-bar verses. There's something to be said for spacing out the lines, to infiltrate people's minds.

Drake, on crafting his live performances for his audiences, interview with Michael Paterniti, *GQ*, June 18, 2013.

I haven't met somebody that makes everybody else not matter.

Drake, on his ongoing relationship status,* interview with Jonah Weiner, *Rolling Stone*, February 13, 2014.

*Drake has dated several famous women, including Serena Williams, Rihanna, Kylie Jenner, Bella Hadid, Nicki Minaj and Jennifer Lopez.

I spent a lot of years looking in through this glass window, and three years later I became a king. There's no city that I go to that I don't feel appreciated, as far as being accepted in that world, whether it's a club, a strip club, a restaurant.

”

Drake, on fame and success, interview with Damien Scott, *Complex*, November 15, 2011.

I just want to be a time-marker for my generation. Whatever my generation is. I'm 28, but I feel like maybe there's kids right now, who are 16, that might still grow up with Drake.

”

Drake, on his aspirations to inspire future generations, interview with Leon Neyfakh, *Fader*, September 24, 2015.

I can't wait to get back into acting. No one ever asks me to do movies, and, although music is my focal point now, I'd love to do a film. That was the life that I lived before, and it would be interesting to live it again.

Drake, on kickstarting his acting career, interview with Lynn Hirschberg, *W Magazine*, October 15, 2015.

I told myself, I would definitely have a song that strictly belonged to Toronto but that the world embraced. 'Know Yourself' was the first big thing off my checklist.

”

Drake, on giving back to his hometown, interview with Leon Neyfakh, *Fader*, September 24, 2015.

I took the biggest leap ever. It's an unimaginable leap in my mind. Girls are dancing to my music. They want to fuck me. Guys want to dap me up, talk to me. Guys that I don't even know or guys that I respect, like athletes, actors, rappers.

Drake, on finding fame as a rapper after being a child actor, interview with Damien Scott, *Complex*, November 15, 2011.

I can't really write a song unless it's about me. And sometimes I have to allow myself the moments to live a little bit.

Drake, on his lyrical muse, interview with Amos Barshad, *Heeb*, June 18, 2010.

I can do two things – rap and sing – and they both sound good. Not a lot of people can do that.

99

Drake, on being one of the few rappers who can hold a tune, interview with John Jurgensen, *Wall Street Journal*, November 11, 2011.

“Because I shake so many hands and get so much love in a day, when I have to go home and sleep by myself I’m never really tripping anymore, because my desires are fed all day by all of these people on the street I meet.”

Drake, on feeling the love from his fans, interview with Damien Scott, *Complex*, November 15, 2011.

I'm where I truly deserve to be. I believe in myself, in my presence, enough that I don't feel small in Jay-Z's presence.

”

Drake, on believing in himself, interview with Jon Caramanica, *New York Times*, June 9, 2010.

If I don't deliver on this first album it could be the downfall of my entire career.

Drake, on the colossal expectation of his debut album, 2010's *Thank Me Later*, interview with Amos Barshad, *Heeb*, June 18, 2010.

Driving is just one of the most pivotal things in my writing life. Sometimes those drives are heavy, man, depending on what happened where you came from and what's about to happen where you're going.

Drake, on the greatest thing he misses now he's famous, interview with Leon Neyfakh, *Fader*, September 24, 2015.

I love when people get upset and say my music isn't hip-hop. I'm like, 'That's great. You're passionate about something.' I'm not saying I agree with it, but I'm glad to see they're passionate about something.

Drake, on his haters expressing their opinion, interview with Damien Scott, *Complex*, November 15, 2011.

The hand that was dealt to me doesn't exist. I can change that. I can change anything.

Drake, on rising up above his troubled childhood and broken home, interview with Jon Caramanica, *New York Times*, June 9, 2010.